For Jo
DR

For my mom and dad, who met dancing at the Palladium
EV

Thank you to Hilary Van Dusen and Marietta Zacker
for extraordinary guidance.

Text copyright © 2021 by Dean Robbins
Illustrations copyright © 2021 by Eric Velasquez

First edition 2021

Library of Congress Catalog Card Number pending
ISBN 978-1-5362-0608-1

21 22 23 24 25 26 CCP 10 9 8 7 6 5 4 3 2 1

Printed in Shenzhen, Guangdong, China

This book was typeset in Filosofia.
The illustrations were done using oil paint
on hot press watercolor paper.

Candlewick Press
99 Dover Street
Somerville, Massachusetts 02144

www.candlewick.com

¡MAMBO Mucho MAMBO!

The Dance That Crossed Color Lines

DEAN ROBBINS
ILLUSTRATED BY ERIC VELASQUEZ

CANDLEWICK PRESS

Millie whirled.
Her arms waved and knees wiggled.
She danced to smooth jazz songs
in her Italian neighborhood.

Trumpets tooted.
Saxophones trilled.
No one danced to jazzy songs
like Millie.

Pedro jumped.

His shoulders jerked and elbows jiggled.

He danced to snappy Latin songs in his Puerto Rican neighborhood.

Maracas rattled.

Congas rumbled.

No one danced to Latin songs like Pedro.

People danced all over New York City in places with live music and lots of space to strut their stuff.

But they had to follow 1940s rules. People from different neighborhoods weren't supposed to mix. Not at dances and not in many other ways.

Italians danced in Italian places.

Puerto Ricans danced in Puerto Rican places.

Black people danced in Black places.

Jews danced in Jewish places.

Then came a band called Machito and His Afro-Cubans. Machito was a percussionist who loved all kinds of music. So did Mario Bauzá, his musical director and trumpeter.

They used jazz trumpets and saxophones, plus Latin maracas and congas, to make a brand-new sound called Latin jazz.

No one had ever heard such
thrilling music! The melodies were
bright and brilliant.
They made you want to listen.
The beats were lilting and lively.
They made you want to move.

Latin jazz was music for the head,
the heart, and the hips.
Everyone danced to it. Italians.
Puerto Ricans. Black people. Jews.
And many others in New York City.

If only there were someplace they
could all dance together.

In 1948, the Palladium Ballroom broke the rules.

Owner Maxwell Hyman opened his doors to all people and hired Machito and His Afro-Cubans to play.

Italians came, like Millie. Puerto Ricans came, like Pedro.
Black people came, like Ernie and Dotty.
Jews came, like Harry and Rose.

And people came from many other neighborhoods. They listened to Machito's bold new music and tried a bold new way to dance.

The Mambo!

Mambo dancers went forward and backward, side to side.

Feet kicked and flicked.
Bodies swiveled and swung.

Machito shouted from the bandstand.

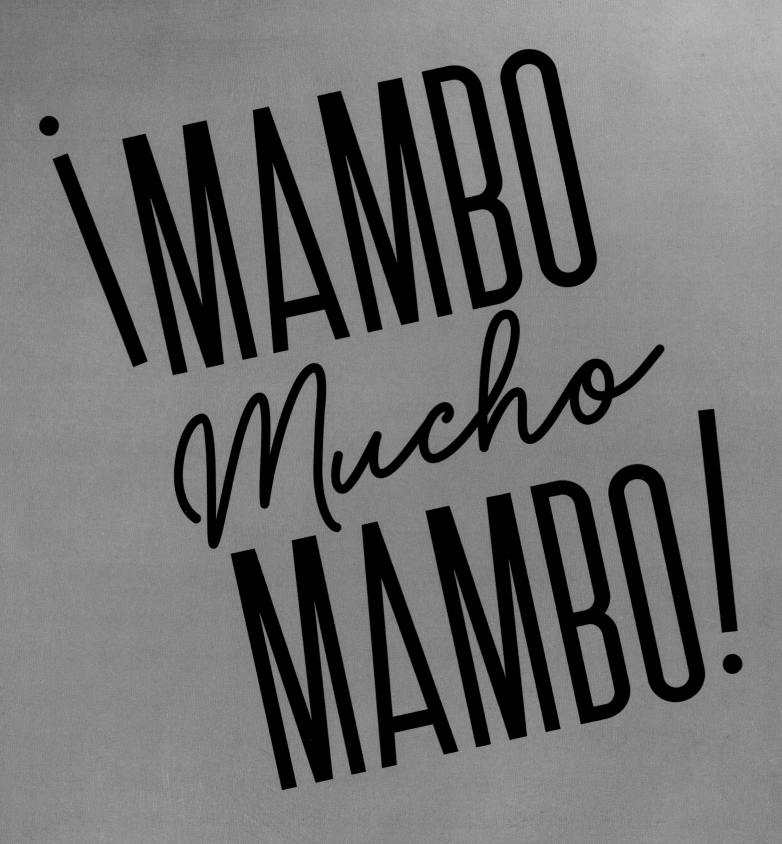

¡MAMBO Mucho MAMBO!

Millie swayed and swirled at one end of the Palladium Ballroom.

Pedro twisted and twirled at the other.

They moved closer . . .

closer . . .

and finally danced together.

"Bravo!" "¡Qué rico!" "So sweet!" "So beautiful!"

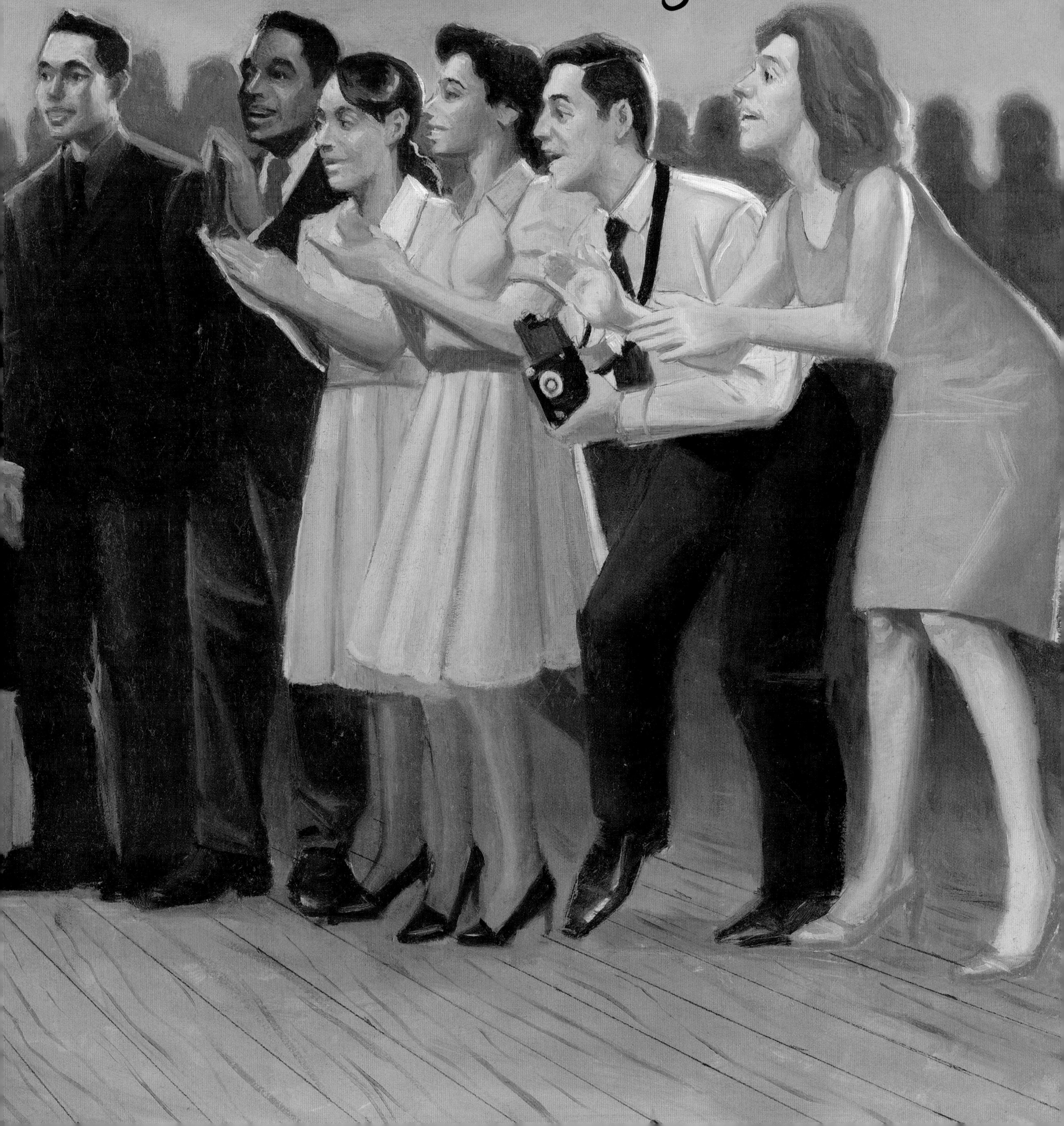

Millie and Pedro made up
mambo moves for two.
Classy, splashy, flashy moves!
The Italian girl and the
Puerto Rican guy became
the best mambo team
in the Palladium.
Then the best in
New York City.
Then the best
in the United States.

Millie and Pedro
showed the world that
anyone, anytime,
anywhere, can
dance together
to Latin jazz.

Author's Note

Machito's real name was Francisco Raúl Gutiérrez Grillo. In 1940, he formed Machito and His Afro-Cubans and helped invent Latin jazz. The band played their songs in the sophisticated jazz style that was popular in the United States, improvising on traditional jazz instruments such as trumpets and saxophones. But they also added strong dancing rhythms from African and Latin American countries, like Machito's native Cuba, along with Latin American instruments such as maracas and congas.

Mario Bauzá, who composed classic songs for Machito and His Afro-Cubans, compared the music to the layers of a lemon meringue pie: jazz on top and Afro-Cuban rhythms on the bottom. It blended influences from many cultures.

Machito, Tito Puente, Tito Rodríguez, and other great Latin jazz bandleaders started in a part of New York City called Spanish Harlem, becoming popular with the neighborhood's many Latino residents. They soon took their music three miles south to the Palladium Ballroom, which welcomed fans from all neighborhoods. The diverse audience at the Palladium marveled over the wide range of expression in Latin jazz, from elegance to ecstasy. I saw Puente's band late in his career and swooned over the joyous music, just like the people who first heard it in the 1940s.

Latin jazz was thought-provoking for those who paid close attention to the creative compositions and solos. It was deeply emotional for those who responded to the passionate performances. And it was fun to dance to for those who just wanted to cut loose.

The new Latin jazz style paired perfectly with a new dance, the mambo, which came from Cuba. During songs like "Mambo Mucho Mambo," dancers moved to the powerful beat, stepping quickly while swinging their hips in a smooth motion. Each couple added their own ideas, from leaps to backbends to splits.

Some of the Palladium dancers became well known for their special talents. Ernie Ensley and Dotty Adams did wild jumps and spins that many others tried to imitate. Harry and Rose Fine danced while Harry worked as the ballroom's photographer. Harry sometimes took pictures as he did the mambo, sliding across the floor on his knees!

Millie Donay won a dance contest at the Palladium in 1950, and so did Pedro Aguilar. They met at the ballroom, married, and became one of the country's best mambo teams. As a mixed-race couple, they also challenged the prejudice of the times. Few people had seen a white woman and a man of color proudly dancing together in public.

By challenging segregation, the Palladium Ballroom set the stage for the 1950s civil rights movement. In the 1960s, the movement succeeded in changing the laws of the United States so that people of all backgrounds could mix on the dance floor and everywhere else.

Resources

Acosta, Leonardo. *Cubano Be, Cubano Bop: One Hundred Years of Jazz in Cuba*. Washington, DC: Smithsonian Books, 2003.

Collier, James Lincoln. *The Making of Jazz*. New York: Dell, 1978.

Fernandez, Raul A. *From Afro-Cuban Rhythms to Latin Jazz*. Berkeley: University of California Press, 2006.

Leymarie, Isabelle. *Cuban Fire: The Story of Salsa and Latin Jazz*. New York: Continuum, 2002.

Machito and His Afro-Cuban Orchestra. *Mambo Mucho Mambo: The Complete Columbia Masters*. Sony, 2002, CD.

"Mambo Dance Steps Online." www.learntodance.com/mambo-dance-lessons/.

McCabe, Daniel, dir. *Latin Music USA*. Episode 1, "Bridges." Aired October 13, 2009, on PBS. www.pbs.org/wgbh/latinmusicusa/home/.

McMains, Juliet. Palladium-Mambo.com. www.palladium-mambo.com.

Puente, Tito. *The Essential Tito Puente*. Sony Legacy, 2005, CD.

Rodríguez, Tito. *The Best of Tito Rodríguez & His Orchestra*, vols. 1 and 2. Sony US Latin, 2004, CD.

Roy, Maya. *Cuban Music: From Son and Rumba to the Buena Vista Social Club and Timba Cubana*. Princeton, NJ: Markus Wiener, 2002.

Salazar, Max. *Mambo Kingdom: Latin Music in New York*. New York: Schirmer, 2002.

Sublette, Ned. *Cuba and Its Music: From the First Drums to the Mambo*. Chicago: Chicago Review Press, 2004.